12 INCREDIBLE FACTS ABOUT THE
MONTGOMERY BUS BOYCOTT

by Lois Sepahban

12 STORY LIBRARY

www.12StoryLibrary.com

12-Story Library is an imprint of Peterson Publishing Company and Press Room Editions.

Produced for 12-Story Library by Red Line Editorial

Photographs ©: Bettmann/Corbis, cover, 1, 11, 17, 21, 23, 28; Warren K. Leffler/Library of Congress, 4, 24; Jack Delano/Library of Congress, 5; The George F. Landegger Collection of Alabama Photographs/Carol M. Highsmith's America/Library of Congress, 6; Neftali/Shutterstock Images, 7; Herman Hiller/Library of Congress, 8; Horace Cort/AP Images, 9; Everett Historical/Shutterstock Images, 10; AP Images, 12, 26; Dick DeMarsico/Library of Congress/©1964 Dr. Martin Luther King, Jr. © renewed 1992 Coretta Scott King, 13; Gene Herrick/AP Images/©1955 Dr. Martin Luther King, Jr. © renewed 1983 Coretta Scott King, 15; Pete Spiro/Shutterstock Images, 16; Rob Carr/AP Images, 18; Joseph Sohm/Shutterstock Images, 19, 29; Gene Herrick/AP Images, 20, 25; Hulton-Deutsch Collection/Corbis, 22; The Lyda Hill Texas Collection of Photographs/Carol M. Highsmith's America/Library of Congress, 27

ISBN
978-1-63235-132-6 (hardcover)
978-1-63235-175-3 (paperback)
978-1-62143-227-2 (hosted ebook)

Library of Congress Control Number: 2015933986

Printed in the United States of America
Mankato, MN
June, 2015

Go beyond the book. Get free, up-to-date content on this topic at 12StoryLibrary.com.

TABLE OF CONTENTS

Segregation Laws Rule the South 4

Rosa Parks Says "No" 6

The Popular South Jackson Line Is Empty 8

Montgomery Police Follow Buses 10

Martin Luther King Jr. Takes a Stand 12

Black Community Continues Bus Boycott 14

Rolling Churches Drive Boycotters to Work 16

Bus Line Refuses Boycott Demands 18

The White Citizens Council Opposes Boycott 20

KKK Violence Erupts in Montgomery 22

Grand Jury Indicts Community Leaders 24

Bus Boycotters Lead the Way to Civil Rights 26

12 Key Dates 28

Glossary 30

For More Information 31

Index 32

About the Author 32

SEGREGATION LAWS RULE THE SOUTH

In 1868, the 14th Amendment to the United States Constitution became law. It said that all citizens, including former slaves, had the right to be protected by US laws. But many white people in the South did not agree. They passed laws of their own. These laws forced black people to live separately from white people. Black people could not use the same schools, restaurants, or bathrooms as white people. This kind of separation is called segregation. Southern states with segregation laws included

Some taxicabs served only white passengers.

White Only 20

Beck's CABS

HE 6-2424·6-1515

CLAUDETTE COLVIN

On March 2, 1955, 15-year-old Claudette Colvin took a stand. She refused to give up her seat for white passengers in Montgomery. The bus driver called the police. Colvin was dragged off the bus and arrested. A judge convicted her of assaulting the police. She was one of several young black people who challenged segregation laws by refusing to give up their seats on buses.

COLORED
WAITING ROOM

PRIVATE PROPERTY
NO PARKING
Driving through or Turning Around

Some bus stations had separate waiting rooms.

Alabama, Arkansas, Georgia, Florida, Louisiana, Mississippi, North Carolina, South Carolina, Tennessee, Texas, and Virginia.

Segregation laws were based on skin color. They discriminated against black people and other racial minorities. Black people did not have the same rights and opportunities as white people.

In Montgomery, Alabama, the city bus line was segregated. The first ten rows of seats were saved for white people only. Black people had to sit behind those seats. Sometimes, the bus became crowded and there were more white people than could fit into the first rows. When that happened, the bus driver moved black people even farther to the back of the bus. Black people without seats were told to stand. They had to give their seats to white people.

36
Number of seats on a Montgomery city bus.

- Segregation laws were common in the South.
- Segregation limited the rights and opportunities of black people and other racial minorities.
- Montgomery's city bus line was segregated. Black people had to sit in the back of the bus or stand.

ROSA PARKS SAYS "NO"

In 1955, Rosa Parks was a 42-year-old black woman living in Montgomery, Alabama. She worked as a seamstress. She was also involved in the National Association for the Advancement of Colored People (NAACP). This organization worked to gain equal rights for black people.

December 1, 1955, started off as a typical day for Parks. She paid

The exact spot where Rosa Parks waited for her bus

JO ANN ROBINSON

Jo Ann Robinson was a professor at Alabama State College. She was also a member of the Women's Political Council. In 1949, she accidentally sat in the white section of a bus. The bus driver shouted at her, and she got off the bus. That day, she vowed to do whatever she could to end bus segregation.

2013

USA FOREVER

Rosa Parks

A stamp celebrates Rosa Parks.

Cost, in cents, for a ride on the Montgomery bus line in 1955.

- On December 1, 1955, Rosa Parks refused to give up her seat on a bus in Montgomery, Alabama.
- Parks was arrested for her actions.
- Other black community leaders planned to boycott buses in Montgomery.

10 cents to ride the bus home after work. She sat behind the sign on the bus that separated white passengers from black passengers.

After the white section of the bus filled, the driver told Parks and the other three black passengers sitting in her row to stand up so that a white man could sit there. The other passengers in her row moved to the back, but Parks stayed in her seat. The bus driver walked to the back of the bus. He asked Parks if she was going to get up. She told him no. The driver called the police. Parks

was taken off the bus and arrested.

Parks's arrest was the final straw for the frustrated black citizens of Montgomery. That night, Jo Ann Robinson from the Women's Political Council wrote a letter to the black community. It encouraged everyone to boycott buses for one day on Monday, December 5. At the same time, E. D. Nixon, the founder of the Montgomery NAACP, was busy calling local pastors and black community leaders. He asked them to support the boycott.

THE POPULAR SOUTH JACKSON LINE IS EMPTY

During the weekend following Rosa Parks's arrest, the Montgomery black community made plans for Monday's boycott. The letter from the Women's Political Council asked people to walk, share rides, or take taxis if they had to go to work. On Sunday, December 4, pastors from local black churches encouraged their church members to support the bus boycott. On Monday morning, citizens of Montgomery watched to see what would happen.

The South Jackson line was a bus route. It was usually full of black women. They rode the bus from their homes to the big houses where they were maids for white families. On the morning of December 5, Coretta Scott King, the wife of Martin Luther King Jr., watched for the bus from her window. The first bus to drive by was empty. The buses that followed it were also empty.

Coretta Scott King

8

The boycott left many Montgomery buses empty of passengers.

95

Approximate percent of the Montgomery black community that took part in the bus boycott on December 5.

- Black community and church leaders encouraged people to participate in the bus boycott.
- Coretta Scott King saw empty South Jackson line buses drive past her house.
- People took taxis, carpooled, or walked to work instead of riding the buses.

Despite the cold December weather, people were staying off the bus. They took taxis, carpooled, and even walked to work. It looked like the bus boycott was going to happen.

THINK ABOUT IT

How do you think Coretta Scott King felt when she saw the buses empty? How would you feel in her position?

MONTGOMERY POLICE FOLLOW BUSES

Montgomery government and law enforcement officials wanted to stop the boycott. Many held racist ideas about black people. They did not believe black people should have the same rights as white people. They wanted segregation to continue.

Montgomery Police Commissioner Clyde Sellers sent messages out on the radio. In the messages, he claimed that some black people were being forced to stay off the buses. He said other black people were intimating these people. He claimed that groups of violent black people were ready to hurt any black person who tried to ride the bus.

No one in the black community had seen violence or received threats from other black people. But still, Sellers sent armed police officers to follow the buses. He said that the police officers would keep any black people who wanted to ride the bus safe. But when black people saw armed police officers following the

WAITING ROOM FOR COLORED ONLY.

← BY ORDER POLICE DEPT.

Some people wanted segregation to continue.

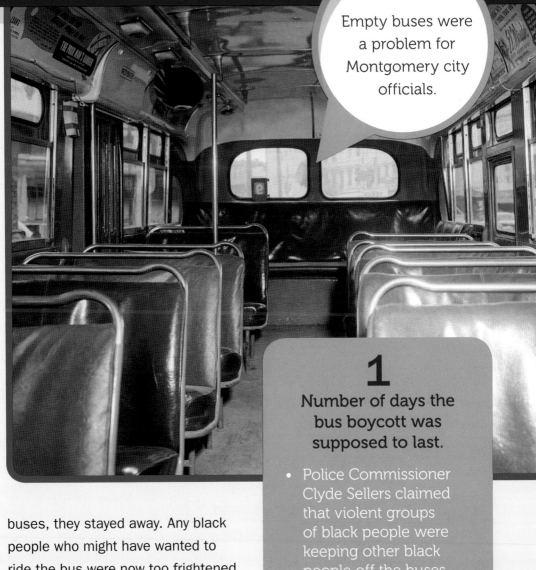

Empty buses were a problem for Montgomery city officials.

buses, they stayed away. Any black people who might have wanted to ride the bus were now too frightened by the police to do so.

Sellers also wanted his police officers to make arrests during the boycott. But they could not find anyone to arrest. Boycotters were peacefully staying off the buses.

1
Number of days the bus boycott was supposed to last.

- Police Commissioner Clyde Sellers claimed that violent groups of black people were keeping other black people off the buses.
- Sellers had police cars follow the buses.
- Black people who might have wanted to ride the bus stayed away because of the police presence.
- Police officers did not find any groups of violent black people to arrest.

MARTIN LUTHER KING JR. TAKES A STAND

Martin Luther King Jr. was 26 years old in December 1955. He was the pastor of the Dexter Avenue Baptist Church in Montgomery. King was newly married and had a baby daughter.

On Monday, December 5, King, other local pastors, and black community leaders met to decide whether to keep the bus boycott going.

Many people present did not want to continue the boycott. They worried that it would anger the white people who governed Montgomery. Many of the leaders worried that they could be arrested or even attacked if they publically stood up in favor of the boycott. They worried about the impact on their families.

When NAACP leader E. D. Nixon asked who was brave enough to

E. D. Nixon (center) with Rosa Parks and her attorney

E. D. NIXON

E. D. Nixon was the founder of the Montgomery chapter of the NAACP. It was his idea to use Rosa Parks's arrest to help overturn the segregation laws in the South. He was at the meeting on December 5, 1955, when the MIA was formed.

stand up for the boycott, King spoke up. He said he wasn't afraid to support the boycott. The rest of the community leaders followed King's lead. The boycott would continue.

That night, they created the Montgomery Improvement Association (MIA). The purpose of the MIA was to organize the boycott. King was elected the MIA's first president.

75
Percent of Montgomery bus riders who were black.

- King was a young pastor in Montgomery.
- Some community leaders feared the consequences of continuing the bus boycott.
- King wanted to stand up for the rights of all black people.
- The Montgomery Improvement Association (MIA) was created to organize the boycott. King was made the group's president.

Dr. Martin Luther King Jr.

THINK ABOUT IT

Community leaders in Montgomery worried about continuing the boycott. What were the leaders worried about? Use the information from these pages to support your answer.

BLACK COMMUNITY CONTINUES BUS BOYCOTT

The night of December 5, members of the black community gathered at Holt Street Baptist Church for a rally to support Rosa Parks. The MIA and other black community leaders hoped the boycott would continue. But the boycott would only go on if the black community supported it.

At least 5,000 people attended the rally that night. The large crowd could not fit inside the church. Loudspeakers delivered messages to the people who were outside.

King spoke to the crowd. His job was to persuade them to continue the boycott. He knew that many people were not excited to continue the bus boycott. Many people did not have cars to drive to work. These people would have to walk to work and back. They would have to worry about being outside in poor weather.

In his speech, King told his listeners that it was time to stand up against oppression. He told them it was their responsibility. He asked them to join him in a nonviolent protest. That night, the vote to continue the bus boycott was unanimous. Everyone voted to support it.

15

Number of minutes the ovation for King lasted after his speech at Holt Street Baptist Church.

- At least 5,000 people attended the rally.
- King's speech encouraged people to stand up against injustice.
- The vote to continue the bus boycott was unanimous.

ROLLING CHURCHES DRIVE BOYCOTTERS TO WORK

Many of those who supported the bus boycott had to travel many miles to get to work. Some were able to walk long distances, but it was difficult for others. During the first week of the boycott, taxicab drivers pitched in to help.

Taxicab drivers who supported the boycott lowered their fares from the normal 45 cents to 10 cents per ride. The city of Montgomery had a rule that required taxi drivers to charge at least 45 cents. But many drivers wanted to help boycotters. Police Commissioner Sellers said that any taxi driver who didn't charge at least 45 cents would be arrested. The taxicab army lasted only for one week.

After that, the MIA found a new way to help boycotters. It organized a carpool system to take boycotters to and from work. The first night, approximately 150 cars were signed up to drive boycotters. When car owners signed up their cars for the carpool, they agreed to let other people take turns driving their cars. Most of the carpool drivers were black

For one week, taxicab drivers lowered their fares to 10 cents to help the boycotters.

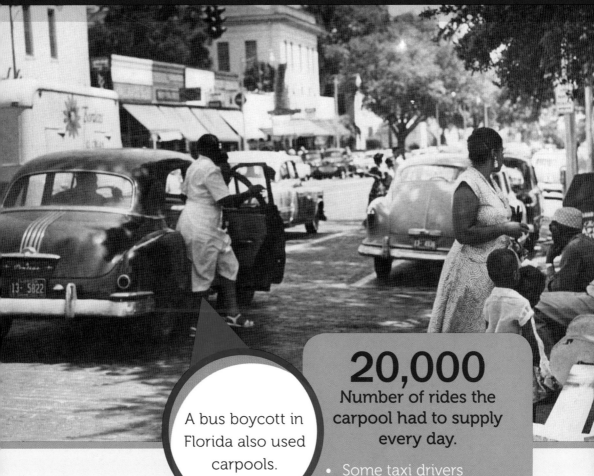

A bus boycott in Florida also used carpools.

20,000

Number of rides the carpool had to supply every day.

citizens, but some white people who supported the boycott donated their cars.

The MIA received donations from groups around the country too. Some of those donations were used to buy more cars. Churches also donated cars. They painted their church names on the sides of their cars. They became known as "rolling churches."

- Some taxi drivers lowered their fees to drive bus boycotters for only 10 cents.
- Montgomery police threatened to arrested taxi drivers who were not charging at least 45 cents for rides.
- Car owners signed up their cars for a carpool to help boycotters get to work.
- Churches donated cars, which became known as "rolling churches."

BUS LINE REFUSES BOYCOTT DEMANDS

The boycott had an immediate effect on the city bus line. The buses had to drive their routes even if no one rode the buses. Without black riders, the city bus line was losing at least $400 per day.

On December 8, 1955, the Montgomery city commission decided to meet with the MIA. The city wanted the group to end the boycott. The MIA had several demands. The MIA wanted the bus line to treat black riders with courtesy. They asked that the bus

In 2005, Robert Graetz speaks about his involvement in the boycott.

ROBERT GRAETZ

Reverend Robert Graetz was the white minister of Trinity Lutheran Church, an all-black church. He and his family supported the bus boycott. They participated in the carpool system. His house was bombed three times because of his support of the boycott.

The MIA wanted to change the bus seating rules.

line hire black drivers for bus routes in black neighborhoods. And they wanted the bus line to end the practice of forcing black passengers to give up their seats for white passengers. They wanted seating to be determined on a first-come, first-seated basis.

The lawyer for the city commission said that the bus company would not agree to the terms. The lawyer said that would be against segregation laws. The boycott would continue.

3
Number of demands outlined by the bus boycotters.

- The Montgomery city bus line lost money because of the boycott.
- The MIA demanded that the city treat black passengers with courtesy, hire black bus drivers, and end segregation of bus seating.
- The city would not agree to the MIA's demands. The boycott continued.

9

THE WHITE CITIZENS COUNCIL OPPOSES BOYCOTT

The White Citizens Council was an organization of white business and community leaders in Montgomery. They wanted segregation to continue. They told white people that they should protest the bus boycott by riding buses themselves. They wanted white people who usually drove their own cars to ride buses instead. They hoped this would make the boycott less effective.

Montgomery Mayor W. A. Gayle joined the White Citizens Council. The Montgomery city commissioners also joined the White Citizens Council. They claimed that Martin Luther King was just causing trouble.

Mayor Gayle and the city commissioners wanted to arrest King and other black community leaders.

W. A. Gayle

17

Number of tickets Jo Ann Robinson got for driving a carpool in 1956.

- The White Citizens Council tried to make up for the bus boycott by asking white people with cars to take the bus instead.
- Montgomery police were told to ticket black people driving carpools for anything they could think of.
- King was arrested for going five miles per hour more than the speed limit.

They hoped doing so would end the boycott. They told police to stop carpool drivers and give them tickets for anything they could think of. They told police to arrest boycotters who rode in carpools for hitchhiking.

On January 26, 1956, King was pulled over. He was arrested for driving 30 miles per hour. The speed limit was 25 miles per hour.

KKK VIOLENCE ERUPTS IN MONTGOMERY

The Ku Klux Klan (KKK) is a white supremacist organization. In 1956, the KKK wanted to stop the bus boycott. Members of the KKK supported segregation. They had racist views about black people.

At the beginning of the boycott, KKK members began harassing boycotters. They called King's house and shouted profanities at whomever answered the phone. They wrote notes telling him to leave town.

On January 31, 1956, a bomb was thrown into King's house. His wife and baby daughter were in the house when the bomb exploded. Luckily, they were not hurt. During the night of February 1, dynamite was thrown into E. D. Nixon's yard, but no one was hurt.

The KKK tried to use violence and threats to scare boycotters.

Boycott leader Reverend Ralph Abernathy (right) had his home bombed after the boycott.

These attacks made people angry and fearful. But King and other black leaders reminded boycotters that their protest must be peaceful. They believed that nonviolent protest would prevail. Meanwhile, the KKK and other groups continued to try to use violence to end the boycott.

THINK ABOUT IT

The houses of many bus boycott leaders were bombed. Imagine your house was bombed because of your participation in the bus boycott. Would you have continued boycotting? Why or why not?

7

Number of men arrested on January 30, 1957, for several bombings and attempted bombings related to the boycott.

- Trying to put an end to the boycott, KKK members harassed boycotters.
- A bomb was tossed into King's house.
- Dynamite exploded in E. D. Nixon's yard.

GRAND JURY INDICTS COMMUNITY LEADERS

The boycott and the KKK violence worried Montgomery city leaders. Judge Eugene Carter set up a grand jury to investigate. He wanted the grand jury to find out if the boycott was illegal.

On February 21, 1956, the grand jury indicted 115 people for the boycott. That means that they were charged with a crime. The grand jury said that a 1921 Alabama

Ralph Abernathy

BOYCOTTERS ON TRIAL

The only person to go on trial for arrest during the boycott was Martin Luther King Jr. His trial was on March 19, 1956. He was found guilty of breaking the law. His punishment was to pay $500 or to serve one year of hard labor. He appealed but lost. He was forced to pay the fine.

$300

The bond that each person arrested agreed to pay if he or she didn't return for trial.

- On February 21, 1956, a grand jury claimed that boycotts were illegal in Alabama.
- The grand jury charged 115 people for the boycott.
- Many boycotters turned themselves in the next day.

law said that boycotts were illegal. The grand jury claimed the bus boycotters were breaking the law.

Those who were indicted included all of the carpool drivers and King, Nixon, Parks, Robinson, and Reverend Ralph Abernathy. City leaders told them the charges would be dropped if the boycott stopped.

The next morning, those who were indicted began turning themselves in. Members of the black community gathered in front of the courthouse to support those who were arrested. Being arrested became a source of pride.

Parks was fingerprinted after she turned herself in.

BUS BOYCOTTERS LEAD THE WAY TO CIVIL RIGHTS

Good news came on June 19, 1956. A federal court ruled that segregation on buses was unconstitutional. It ordered Montgomery to end segregation on the buses. But lawyers for the city of Montgomery asked the Supreme Court to look at the case. While they waited for the Supreme Court to make a decision, the boycott continued.

On November 13, the US Supreme Court made a decision. The Supreme Court ruled in favor of the boycotters. The Supreme Court said that any person, regardless of skin color, could sit on any open seat on any bus. But city of Montgomery still didn't want to give in. Lawyers for the city asked the Supreme Court to rethink its decision. That process would take another month.

Two black men sit at the front of the bus after bus segregation was ruled unconstitutional.

381

Number of days the Montgomery bus boycott lasted.

- The court case that was taken to the Supreme Court was called *Browder v. Gayle*.
- The Supreme Court ruled that bus segregation was illegal.
- The Montgomery bus boycott launched the civil rights moment.

until justice rolls down
like waters
and righteousness
like a mighty stream

Dr. Martin Luther King, Jr.

A statue of Rosa Parks in Dallas, Texas

In spite of this, members of the black community of Montgomery held a rally to celebrate the Supreme Court's decision. While the black community continued to boycott and waited for the Supreme Court decision to be final, King reminded those around him that peaceful protest worked. He encouraged them to use peaceful protests to fight for civil rights throughout the South.

On December 20, 1956, the Supreme Court told the city of Montgomery that its decision was final. The next morning, King, Abernathy, Graetz, and other leaders boarded a city bus. Montgomery city buses were officially desegregated. The boycott was officially over.

The Montgomery bus boycott was the beginning of the civil rights movement. It led to other nonviolent protests throughout the South to end segregation. There were more bombings, beatings, arrests, and even murders by the opposition. But nonviolent protesters continued to fight for equal rights for all people.

12 KEY DATES

December 1, 1955
Rosa Parks is arrested for not giving up her seat on a Montgomery city bus.

December 4, 1955
Pastors and community leaders encourage the black community to boycott buses.

December 5, 1955
The bus boycott begins.

December 8, 1955
The MIA and the Montgomery city commission negotiates to end the boycott but do not come to an agreement.

January 26, 1956
Martin Luther King Jr. is arrested for speeding.

January 31, 1956
King's house is bombed.

February 1, 1956
Dynamite is thrown into E. D. Nixon's yard.

February 21, 1956
Montgomery grand jury indicts 115 black community leaders.

February 22, 1956
Indicted community leaders turn themselves in at the courthouse.

June 19, 1956

A federal court rules that bus segregation in Alabama is illegal.

November 13, 1956

The US Supreme Court rules that bus segregation in Alabama is illegal.

December 21, 1956

Black community leaders board Montgomery city buses. The boycott is over.

GLOSSARY

assault
An attack.

boycott
To refuse to purchase a good or service as a way of protesting.

chapter
A local branch of an organization.

civil rights
Personal freedoms guaranteed to US citizens.

discriminate
To treat some people better than others without a good reason.

hitchhike
To get a free ride.

indict
To formally determine that a person should be put on trial.

nonviolent
Peaceful, without violence.

oppression
To hold power over an individual or group.

persuade
To win over to a belief.

racist
Having the belief that some races are superior to others.

seamstress
A woman who does sewing work.

segregation
The separation of a race or group of people.

supremacist
A person who believes in the superiority of a particular group, often determined by race or gender.

FOR MORE INFORMATION

Books

Bader, Bonnie. *Who Was Martin Luther King, Jr.?* New York: Grosset & Dunlap, 2008.

Freedman, Russell. *Freedom Walkers: The Story of the Montgomery Bus Boycott.* New York: Holiday House, 2010.

Jeffrey, Gary. *Rosa Parks and the Montgomery Bus Boycott.* New York: Gareth Stevens, 2013.

Kimmel, Allison Crotzer. *The Montgomery Bus Boycott.* North Mankato, MN: Capstone, 2015.

Websites

DuSable Museum of African American History
www.dusablemuseum.org/exhibits/details/381-days-the-montgomery-bus-boycott-story

The Henry Ford Museum: The Rosa Parks Bus
www.thehenryford.org/exhibits/rosaparks/home.asp

National Civil Rights Museum: The Year They Walked
www.civilrightsmuseum.org/project/the-year-they-walked

INDEX

Abernathy, Ralph, 25, 27

Browder v. Gayle, 27

carpools, 9, 16–17, 18, 21, 25,
Carter, Eugene, 24
Colvin, Claudette, 4

Dexter Avenue Baptist Church, 12

Gayle, W. A., 20
Graetz, Robert, 18, 27,

Holt Street Baptist Church, 14

King, Coretta Scott, 8–9
King, Martin Luther, Jr., 8, 12–13, 14, 20, 21, 22–23, 24, 25, 27
Ku Klux Klan (KKK), 22–23, 24

Montgomery Improvement Association (MIA), 12, 13, 14, 16–17, 18–19
Montgomery police, 4, 7, 10–11, 21

National Association for the Advancement of Colored People (NAACP), 6, 7, 12
Nixon, E. D., 7, 12, 22, 25

Parks, Rosa, 6–7, 8, 12, 14, 25

Robinson, Jo Ann, 6, 7, 25

segregation laws, 4–5, 12, 19, 26
Sellers, Clyde, 10–11, 16

taxis, 8, 9, 16

White Citizens Council, 20–21
Women's Political Council, 6, 7, 8

About the Author

Lois Sepahban has written several books for children, including science and history, biography, and fiction. She lives in Kentucky with her husband and two children.

READ MORE FROM 12-STORY LIBRARY

Every 12-Story Library book is available in many formats, including Amazon Kindle and Apple iBooks. For more information, visit your device's store or 12StoryLibrary.com.